Overcoming Sinful Anger

Rev. T. G. Morrow

Overcoming Sinful Anger

How to Master Your Emotions and Bring Peace to Your Life

SOPHIA INSTITUTE PRESS

Manchester, New Hampshire

Sophia Institute Press
Box 5284, Manchester, NH 03108
1-800-888-9344

www.SophiaInstitute.com

Sophia Institute Press® is a registered trademark of Sophia Institute.

Library of Congress Cataloging-in-Publication Data

Morrow, T. G.
    Overcoming sinful anger : how to master your emotions and bring peace
to your life / Rev. T. G. Morrow.
        pages cm
    Includes bibliographical references.
    ISBN 978-1-62282-230-0 (pbk. : alk. paper) 1. Anger—Religious
aspects—Christianity. I. Title.
    BV4627.A5M67 2014
    241'.3—dc23

                                                            2014036024

9th printing

To Mary, Queen of Peace

Contents

Overcoming Sinful Anger

Introduction

Years back a husband told me that his wife said to him one evening when she was feeling stressed, "Get me a glass of wine." He replied, "Would you want to ask that question more politely?"

"No, I wouldn't. Now get me some wine," she responded.

"You need to say *please*," he asserted.

She proceeded to yell and scream and break just about everything in the room until he relented and went to get her a glass of wine. Within a week they were on the verge of separating.

I told him that what he did was a big mistake. "Now she will think that all she has to do to get you to do something is throw a tantrum. The next time she acts like that, I want you to say, 'I need to go for a walk. I'll be back in a half hour.' Then go out and walk around the block until you think she might have calmed down."

Overcoming Sinful Anger

I told his wife that she was using anger to manipulate her husband. I also told her what I had told him, and I suggested that she try to get him to do things by love, not by anger.

Both took the advice, and things got better and better. They had three more children, and they are happily married today.[1]

Anger can be a terrible thing in marriage and in just about every other relationship. By this I mean the capital sin of anger. I propose to distinguish herein between the feeling of anger and the sinful anger that should be overcome.

In the pages that follow, I will try to analyze the dynamics of sinful anger and what God has said about it in Scripture. And, thanks to a recently published book on changing one's behavior, I will offer some ideas, which I consider quite novel, on how to avoid angry explosions.

[1] This is a true story, but some details have been changed to protect the privacy of those involved.

1

Recognize Sinful Anger

"Anger as a deadly sin is 'a disorderly outburst of emotion connected with the inordinate desire for revenge.' . . . It is likely to be accompanied by surliness of heart, by malice aforethought, and above all by the determination to take vengeance."[2] The *Catechism of the Catholic Church* contains a similar description:

> By recalling the commandment, "You shall not kill," our Lord asked for peace of heart and denounced murderous anger and hatred as immoral.
>
> *Anger* is a desire for revenge. "To desire vengeance in order to do evil to someone who should be punished is illicit," but it is praiseworthy to impose

---

[2] Henry Fairlie, *The Seven Deadly Sins Today* (University of Notre Dame Press, 1979), 88.

restitution "to correct vices and maintain justice." If anger reaches the point of a deliberate desire to kill or seriously wound a neighbor, it is gravely against charity; it is a mortal sin. The Lord says, "Everyone who is angry with his brother shall be liable to judgment." (no. 2302)

This is different from the *feeling* of anger, which is not sinful in itself. That anger is defined as "a strong feeling of displeasure or hostility." We can't control when we will feel angry, since that depends on events that occur outside of us. But we can control what we do about the feeling.

As the *Catechism of the Catholic Church* teaches, the feeling of anger is one of the passions. "In the passions, as movements of the sensitive appetite, there is neither moral good nor evil. But insofar as they engage reason and will, there is moral good or evil in them" (no. 1773). So it is how we act based on this feeling that determines whether we sin or not. We find also in the *Catechism* that we should be moved to do good not only by our will but by our heart as well. In other words, we must attempt to convert our very feelings to be fully virtuous (no. 1775).

St. Paul mentions outbursts of anger along with several other sins, including fornication, jealousy, enmity, and strife. He concludes with this warning: "I warn you as I warned you before, that those who do such things will not inherit the kingdom of God" (Gal. 5:20–21). What could be further from Christ's command in the Sermon on the Mount, to "love your enemies and pray for those who persecute you" (Matt. 5:43)? He said, "I say to you that every one who is angry with his brother shall be liable to judgment; whoever insults his brother shall be liable to the council, and whoever says, 'You fool!' shall be liable to the fire of hell" (Matt. 5:22).

We can suppress our anger; or we can express it by sabotaging the efforts of those who caused it; or we can express it in an irrational tirade of bad words and insults; or we can express our anger rationally — or at least process it rationally. If we merely suppress an angry feeling, it will go down into our subconscious and wait for a chance to explode. And it *will* explode. It is better to do something constructive with it.

First, let's consider the dysfunctional ways of dealing with the feeling of anger, the sinful ways.

Passive-Aggressive Behavior

The first tactic in angry people is often passive-aggressive behavior. This is the way the saboteur operates. He is angry but does not show it directly. Instead, he shuts down. He agrees to do something but never does it. According to Dr. Daniel K. Hall-Flavin of the Mayo Clinic, specific signs and symptoms of passive-aggressive behavior include: resentment and opposition to the demands of others, complaining about feeling underappreciated or cheated, procrastination, stubbornness, inefficiency, memory lapses, sullenness, irritability, and a cynical or hostile attitude.[3]

Another passive-aggressive expression of anger, often mentioned by psychologists, is the silent treatment. The basic idea is "I won't get angry. I'll get even." The silent treatment is something we have all seen. "I won't talk to you because I am unhappy with your behavior." It may be a day, or a week, or even two weeks before the angry person opens up. One husband refused to speak to his wife for two weeks without telling her why. Finally, he admitted that it was because he had seen a spot on the wall by the kitchen table! He thought his wife should have cleaned it.

The silent treatment is a symptom of bad communication skills and immaturity. It usually doesn't solve anything.

[3] Daniel K. Hall-Flavin, "What Is Passive-Aggressive Behavior? What Are Some of the Signs?", Mayo Clinic, July 16, 2013, www.mayoclinic.com/health/passive-aggressive-behavior/AN01563.

Recognize Sinful Anger

Another example of passive-aggressive behavior is to do things we know will irritate the person who has angered us. When I was young, I had an acquaintance who would get me angry. I knew that if I did or said certain things, I could, in turn, get him so upset that he would be ready to cry. However, when I got older and was tempted to do this, I had to stop myself: "You can't do that anymore; you're a Christian." I had thought I was a Christian before, but revenge is not part of the Christian's repertoire, so I had to make a choice: either take revenge or be a Christian. Difficult? Of course. Jesus promised a cross (Matt. 16:24).

Taking revenge is sinful. So, as a first step in overcoming passive-aggressive anger, keep reminding yourself that you want to be a Christian, and therefore you can't take revenge anymore.

Exploding with Anger

We have all encountered people who explode when they feel angry. It baffles me how often this sort of anger rears its ugly head in marriages—even in allegedly *Christian* marriages. The damage done by this behavior is huge. A raging father or mother or child is torture for just about everyone in the family, including the angry one. This is another behavior that's incompatible with being a Christian.

Overcoming Sinful Anger

I am often surprised to discover Christians who pray ardently, who receive the sacraments regularly, who even attend Mass daily, and yet have an anger problem. "If any one thinks he is religious, and does not bridle his tongue but deceives his heart, this man's religion is vain" (James 1:26).

Some even say, "Well, if you're [of ethnicity X], you're going to get angry a lot." Not so! Rather, if you're a Christian, you will work very hard to find a way to cut back on your anger dramatically. For the real Christian, it's not where we're from that counts the most, but where we would like to go one day. Explosive anger is not something you want to have with you when you leave this planet. It will profoundly dampen your ability to enter the Kingdom.

If you have a problem with exploding anger and you want to be a Christian, you absolutely *must* work hard to overcome it. You cannot simply say, "Well, that's me," if you want to be friends with the Lord. Granted, perhaps most angry outbursts are not mortal sins because sufficient reflection is absent. But *choosing* not to strive ardently to overcome hateful outbursts is usually done with full knowledge and deliberate consent of the will and so could well be a mortal sin.[4] As with many serious sins, if we are really

---

[4] For a sin to be *mortal*, three conditions must together be met: "Mortal sin is sin whose object is grave matter

trying to overcome them, we can be close to God. If we are not trying, we can't.

Some seem to think that every family has blowups fairly often. This is not true. I don't ever remember my parents getting angry at each other. They solved their problems without anger. Of course, my mother would get angry at us children, but she never was out of control. She never totally lost her temper, and she never said anything mean. (She *had* to get angry with us at times—but always maintaining her temper—because, as she put it, she had "three only children.") I know many families in which uncontrolled anger is rare or nonexistent.

Perpetual Anger

Another dysfunctional expression of anger is illustrated by those who, filled with bitterness, continually bring up the past sins of others. They may not blow up, but they seem to be always on the verge of doing so.

A wife who intended to leave her husband loaded him down with e-mails enumerating his failures of the past. This she did on the rare occasions when she did communicate with him. What a sad way to live. It's the classic case

---

and which is also committed with full knowledge and deliberate consent" (CCC, no. 1857).

of one who constantly brings up old issues, something just about every book on marriage warns against. "You made me suffer in the past, so I will make you pay for the rest of your life" is the mindset. "Forgiveness? What's that?" this woman's life seemed to express. Strangely she hung on to this constantly angry behavior even while praying and attending daily Mass and receiving Holy Communion. What a complete disconnect with the Christian religion!

I encouraged her husband (converted, reformed, and very prayerful) to remind her that God had forgiven him. It should go without saying that if she wanted God to forgive her, she needed to forgive her husband.

A person like this would do well to meditate long and hard on these words from Ephesians: "Let all bitterness and wrath and anger and clamor and slander be put away from you, with all malice, and be kind to one another, tender-hearted, forgiving one another, as God in Christ forgave you" (Eph. 4:31–32). Even more motivating should be the words of the apostle John: "He who does not love remains in death. Any one who hates his brother is a murderer, and you know that no murderer has eternal life abiding in him" (1 John 3:14–15).

Those who persist in their hatred cannot hope to be anything but miserable. It can even cause them to become ill, as we will see in chapter 4.

2

Understand the Causes
of Angry Behavior

Why do people explode in anger? There are many reasons, but I think the top three are power and control, a refusal to take responsibility, and habit.[5]

Power and Control

Some people explode with anger because they discover they can control others by doing this. "If you don't do what I want, I will make you very uncomfortable by blowing up. Then you will realize that you'd better do what I want or else." It's called manipulation: forcing someone to do what

[5] Adapted from Ron Potter-Efron, *An Emergency Guide to Anger Control* (New York: MJF Books, 1994), 37. The author lists six reasons, but I consider here what I see as the top three.

he doesn't want to do. This, of course, is a childish way to act, and it is ultimately self-defeating. You might control someone today with your anger, but tomorrow that person might no longer put up with your behavior or might not even be around to control.

This is the behavior of the woman in the opening example. She had found that she could get her husband to do what she wanted if she blew up. When he refused to be manipulated in this way, she realized she had to find another way to get him to do things: through love.

Refusal to Take Responsibility

Sometimes we refuse to take responsibility for our anger: "It's not my fault. It's *his* fault. Look what he did!"

The truth is that someone else may well have done something wrong, and our feeling of anger may well be his fault. But our blowing our stack is not his fault. It's our own fault. We are not like animals, which, when provoked, have no choice but to react violently. When we feel angry, we have a choice to act either rationally or irrationally. Only one of these reactions qualifies as a Christian one.

So it would be incorrect to say, "He made me lose my cool." Rather, he made me angry, and I chose to lose my cool. We are responsible for what we do.

Understand the Causes of Angry Behavior

Habit

Some people learned to be angry as children because they were so frustrated with the treatment they received from their parents. Or perhaps they saw their father or mother go wild whenever that parent became angry, and they copied that behavior. They have always behaved this way and are not even aware that they have a choice with regard to anger. So they just keep on going with their angry blowups.

However, we are not stuck with our bad habits. We can overcome them. We start by delaying our response to anger. Then we learn to analyze our feeling, as I will speak of shortly. Next, we exercise self-control to process our anger rationally. It is not easy to overcome a bad habit. But, it can be done (see chapter 7), and it's certainly worth it.

The Two Wolves Inside

One thing is certain: losing one's temper in anger tears apart relationships.

> An old man once said to his grandson, who was angry over an injustice received from a friend, "Let me tell you a story. I too, at times, have felt a great hate for those that have taken so much, with no sorrow for what they do. But hate wears you down and

does not hurt your enemy. It is like taking poison and hoping your enemy will die. I have struggled with these feelings many times."

He went on, "It is as if there are two wolves inside me. One is good and does no harm. He lives in harmony with all around him and does not take offense when no offense was intended. He will fight only when it is right to do so, and in the right way.

"But the other wolf, ah! He is full of anger. The littlest thing will set him into a fit of temper. He fights everyone, all the time, for no reason. He cannot think because his anger and hate are so great.

"Sometimes, it is hard to live with these two wolves inside me, for both of them try to dominate my spirit."

The boy looked intently into his grandfather's eyes and asked, "Which one wins, Grandpa?"

The Grandfather smiled and quietly said, "The one I feed."[6]

If you choose to go crazy every time someone crosses you, you will be feeding the angry wolf inside, and it will

[6] Cherokee legend, "Two Wolves," First People, http://www.firstpeople.us/FP-Html-Legends/TwoWolves-Cherokee.html.

dominate your life. If you choose a different response to your angry feelings, you will begin to live more and more in peace. You will be happier, and so will all your friends and neighbors.

3

Process Anger Rationally

It is possible to express anger by strong measures, as Jesus did in the cleansing of the Temple (John 2:14–17). Scripture also indicates that we can be angry without sinning: "Be angry but do not sin; do not let the sun go down on your anger, and give no opportunity to the devil." (Eph. 4:26–27). And St. Thomas Aquinas wrote, "If one is angry in accordance with right reason, one's anger is deserving of praise."[7]

Nonetheless, the vast majority of angry behavior is sinful, and Scripture warns against it:

Make no friendship with a man given to anger, nor go with a wrathful man, lest you learn his ways and entangle yourself in a snare. (Prov. 22:24–25)

---

[7] St. Thomas Aquinas, *Summa Theologica*, II-IIae, Q. 158 (New York: Benziger Brothers, 1948), 1838.

He who is slow to anger is better than the mighty, and he who rules his spirit [is better] than he who takes a city. (Prov. 16:32)

I say to you that every one who is angry with his brother shall be liable to judgment; whoever insults his brother shall be liable to the council, and whoever says, "You fool!" shall be liable to hell. (cf. Matt. 5:22)

Let no evil talk come out of your mouths, but only such as is good for edifying, as fits the occasion, that it may impart grace to those who hear. And do not grieve the Holy Spirit of God, in whom you were sealed for the day of redemption. Let all bitterness and wrath and anger and clamor and slander be put away from you, with all malice, and be kind to one another, tenderhearted, forgiving one another, as God in Christ forgave you. (Eph. 4:29–32)

So what can you do when you experience the feeling of anger? First, take the time to calm down and figure out why you are angry. Seneca wrote, "The greatest remedy for anger is delay." And Will Rogers opined, "People who fly into a rage always make a bad landing." One of the tactics often recommended is to count to ten before deciding what to do. Better still, say a short prayer before acting.

The next step is to ask yourself if your ~~angry feeling~~ has ~~been caused by~~ something significant. Most angry fights in marriage are caused by trifling things. Often a person will tell me, "I had a big fight with my spouse."

"Do you want to tell me what it was about?" I ask.

"You know, I can't remember. I don't think it was anything important." It was such a trivial thing that the person can't even remember what it was!

So it is extremely important to look at the cause of your feeling ~~and ask yourself:~~ Is this worth fighting about, or is it insignificant? ~~If it's~~ insignificant, you need to brush it off and tell yourself, "That's stupid. ~~Don't waste~~ your effort over that. Forget it. Don't sweat the small stuff."

If the cause *is* worth getting angry about, then you have to consider another question: If you say something diplomatically to the person who has angered you, will it do any good, or will it make things worse? (Don't tell me diplomacy is not your strong point. It's no one's strong point until he begins to work at it.) If it could do some good, then you have to muster the courage to explain gently to the person why you are not happy with his behavior.

Or perhaps use humor to make your point. Arnold Palmer was one of the great golfers of his time and also a great crowd-pleaser. I remember watching him on television as he tried to make an important putt. As he stood over the ball, some people in the gallery were rudely talking and ruining his concentration. I thought, "How's he going to remain the crowd-pleaser now?" He stood up and walked toward the crowd, smiled, and put his finger to his mouth. Was he angry? Probably. But he got his message across without being mean. And he got the crowd to be quiet.

Another example is that of the man who set up a video recorder to tape the final of a great tennis match. Someone else came along and turned off the recorder. The man was angry and wanted to express it. But he didn't want to be nasty, so he wrote the culprit a note saying, "Just wait 'til I catch the guy who turned off the recorder as I was taping the tennis final. Just wait!" The villain saw the humor in the message without being hurt or offended and apologized for his misstep.

One young man kept a bottle of orange juice in the refrigerator at his workplace to drink with his breakfast. One day he noticed that someone was pilfering his juice. He thought of writing a nasty note but decided that it probably wouldn't be effective and wasn't very Christian. So he sat down and started writing: "Dear orange juice thief [he was calling a spade a spade!], you may share my orange juice if you like, but if you do, please let me know how much you want so I can plan ahead." He taped it on the bottle of juice. A couple of days later, he found another note on the bottle: "I would like one glass each day. Thank you very much." (The thief had his own sense of humor!) So the young man bought more orange juice. Happily, in a week or so, the thievery ended!

Offering Up Angry Feeling as a Sacrifice

Now, if it wouldn't do any good to express your displeasure diplomatically (for example, if you've tried several times before and it only made things worse), you need to give your anger to the Lord. Offer this feeling as a sacrifice for sins, and every time the feeling comes back, give it to the Lord again. One thing is certain: you need to try to get rid of anger before you go to sleep at night. Not only do counselors advise, "Don't go to bed angry," but Sacred Scripture also says it: "[D]o not let the sun go down on your anger, and give no opportunity to the devil" (Eph. 4:26–27). Every time you feel the anger, just accept it as part of your cross and move on.

This is not the same as suppressing your anger. Suppressing anger can cause major health problems, including high blood pressure, depression, and headaches. Or it may build up and cause you to explode after a while.

Offering your angry feeling as a sacrifice is not suppressing it but doing something with it. It is making a bad situation into a beneficial one. That is what it means to embrace the cross. We accept our pain to bring about redemption. That is precisely what Jesus did, and we can share in his redemptive mission by offering up our anger.

St. Thérèse of Lisieux said, as she lay dying of tuberculosis, "I could never have believed it was possible to suffer so much.... There are no consolations, not even one! It is because of my desire to save souls."

Furthermore, St. Teresa of Ávila wrote, "When you embrace the cross, you do not feel it." In other words, when you face up to your trials in life — including feelings of anger — they don't seem so bad.

4

Learn to Forgive

If we can forgive others, we can pull the rug out from beneath our anger most of the time. Unforgiveness is the main culprit behind anger. And worse, unforgiveness increases our chances of getting heart disease and cancer.[8]

Furthermore, in the Our Father, Jesus tied our being forgiven to our forgiving others (Matt. 6:9–13). And this is the only part of the Our Father that he elaborates on, saying, "For if you forgive men their trespasses, your heavenly Father also will forgive you; but if you do not forgive men their trespasses, neither will your Father forgive your trespasses" (Matt. 6:14–15).

Forgiveness is one of the most fundamental things we are called to practice as Christians. Unforgiveness is an

---

[8] See, for example, Fred Luskin, *Forgive for Good* (San Francisco: HarperCollins, 2002), 78, 79.

indication that we are not truly in touch with our faith: if we are Christian, we forgive. Must we forgive *immediately*? No, but we shouldn't delay too long to begin the process. It may take time, but in the end, we must do it.

What exactly is forgiveness? First, consider what forgiveness *isn't*. Forgiveness is not condoning or making excuses for someone's bad behavior. It is not forgetting; it is not amnesia. You will still remember what your stepmother did to you, but if you forgive, it won't rile you. Forgiveness is not pardoning an act that was just (for such an act, no forgiveness is needed). It is not just returning to a calm state. It is not a phony "I forgive you" said in order to control people or to pretend that someone has not hurt you or to let go of an imaginary offense. And it is not simply reconciling. Reconciling without forgiving is empty.[9]

Then what is forgiveness? It is giving up all resentment, all desire for revenge, and striving to love the one who hurt you—that is, to work for his good. When you have forgiven someone, you do not wish that person ill, you do not hold a grudge, and you try to manifest kindness to the person when you see him.

[9] Robert D. Enright, Ph.D., *Forgiveness Is a Choice* (Washington, DC: APA Life Tools, 2001), 28–31.

Learn to Forgive

If there is a reasonable chance that it would help, it's usually good to express the fact that the person hurt you and that you forgive him. This can be helpful by bringing closure.

What if the person who has hurt you is not sorry and does not apologize? You should still forgive, so that you find peace in letting the matter go, and you can love the person and wish his good. You need not make him your best friend, but you should not hold a grudge. If the person is likely to do the same thing again, however, it is not wrong to guard yourself against another such incident. You needn't open yourself to ongoing hurts.

Even God will not forgive in a certain sense, unless we are sorry and intend to try to reform. This is why Jesus told his apostles, "If you forgive the sins of any, they are forgiven; if you retain the sins of any, they are retained" (John 20:23). And those who refuse to admit their sins even to the Church are to be treated "as a Gentile and a tax collector" (Matt. 18:17).

Nonetheless, God does not hold grudges. He may withhold some of his blessings as a kind of negative grace, to help us realize we are headed in the wrong direction. But he does that out of love, out of concern for our salvation. Even when God punishes us in this life, he does so for our good. "My son, do not regard lightly the discipline of the

Lord, nor lose courage when you are punished by him. For the Lord disciplines him whom he loves, and chastises every son whom he receives" (Heb. 12:5–6).

God is always ready to forgive us if we repent and try to change, and we must be ready to forgive as well. That is why Jesus told Peter he must forgive seventy times seven times (Matt. 18:21).

Unenforceable Rules

Forgiveness expert Dr. Fred Luskin says that anger and unforgiveness quite often stem from the breaking of our "unenforceable rules." For example, my mother should have loved me, or my husband must be faithful, or my friend should never lie to me. If you make a rule like that and it is broken, you may go wild with anger.

Now all of these "rules" are good and desirable, but you cannot ensure that they will play out in life. You may try to manipulate others into keeping these rules, but ultimately, you are setting yourself up for failure. People are free to choose their actions, and sometimes they choose wrongly.

So, you need to change your rules into desires. I hope my husband will be faithful and my friend will not lie to me. It would have been nice if my mother had loved me, but although she didn't live up to my desires, I will survive. And I won't ruin my peace because she didn't come through as I would have liked.[10]

We must keep in mind the Serenity Prayer:

God, give us grace to accept with serenity the things
that cannot be changed,
Courage to change the things that should be changed,
and the Wisdom to distinguish the one from the other.

There is more to this prayer by Reinhold Niebuhr:

Living one day at a time,
Enjoying one moment at a time,
Accepting hardship as a pathway to peace,
Taking, as Jesus did,
This sinful world as it is,
Not as I would have it,
Trusting that You will make all things right,
If I surrender to Your will,
So that I may be reasonably happy in this life,
And supremely happy with You forever in the next.[11]

---

[10] Dr. Fred Luskin, *Forgive for Good* (New York: Harper-Collins, 2003), 123–136.

[11] The prayer as quoted here is different from the popularized one but appears to be the original. From http://skdesigns.com/internet/articles/prose/niebuhr/serenity_prayer.

Overcoming Sinful Anger

People who play sports are usually able to learn this sort of serenity. The true sportsman says implicitly, "I really want to win this game, but if I lose, it will not be the end of the world. My life will go on." Playing sports is a great way to prepare for the ups and downs of life, because it helps us see the foolishness of the unenforceable rule "We've got to win!"

Long-Term Unforgiveness

Luskin proposes a system for those who have struggled for a long time with unforgiveness.

1. The preliminary step is to take responsibility for how you feel.[12] You cannot let the world dictate to you how you should feel. True, your feelings are often influenced by what takes place around you, but you need not be dominated by those feelings. You can choose to reject harmful feelings and pursue healthy ones.

2. Having done that, refocus your thoughts away from the things that have made you angry to some very positive thoughts. For example, thank God for the beautiful weather or for the ability to read or to buy things you need. Thank him for your spouse or your children or for

[12] Luskin, *Forgive for Good*, 110.

a wonderful day or a magnificent sunset. You might think of people you have forgiven or speak to others about their forgiveness experiences. Or read about those who have forgiven great injustices. Or think about times you were loved or when you loved someone well.[13] These are some things Christians should do often, whether they struggle with unforgiveness or not.

3. Luskin encourages people to refocus their attention from the injustice they endured to a "positive intention." What is it that you really want? Is it the return of a lost love, or is it to have a good, strong relationship with someone? If it is the latter, then it's time to forget the lover who jilted you. You can move on and pursue your real goal.[14]

The point is that unforgiveness makes you focus on the wrong thing—your grievances. Enlist your family and friends to help you overcome this. Ask them to tell you when you overdo your "grievance story." Until you can let go of your grievances completely, set a limit on the time you spend on thinking about them; you might, for instance, give yourself just a few moments each day to reflect on an injustice you endured.[15] By focusing instead

[13] Ibid., 110–116.
[14] Ibid., 148, 149.
[15] See ibid., 173, 174.

on what you really want in life, beyond the unfortunate things that happened in the past, you begin to emerge free from a debilitating negativity and hopelessness. You can get beyond what is holding you back from growing, from finding joy in life again.

Four Stages of Forgiveness

Luskin proposes four stages of forgiveness:

1. Recognize the problem and be angry. (Easy enough!)

2. Do something to diminish your hurt. It may involve trying to see things from the other's perspective or just to assert that the matter was not a big deal.

3. Recall how good it felt to forgive in the past.

4. Make a serious effort not to let yourself be offended by things.[16]

That last stage was made for the true Christian. For example, St. John of the Cross developed his own way to reduce the possibility of being offended. He developed the

[16] See Luskin, *Forgive for Good*, 181–183.

concept of being *nada*, "nothing," in order to serve God and not to expect much from the world. St. Catherine of Siena was given a similar approach by God himself. She asked him one day, "Tell me, Lord, who am I, what am I? Lord, tell me also, who and what are you." He replied, "Daughter, I am who am. You are, who are not."[17] He was reminding her of her nothingness in comparison with him.

St. Francis de Sales pursued the idea of not letting events of the world bother him when he was the bishop of Geneva. Once one of his priests became angry when he was turned down for a position that was beyond his capabilities. In response, the priest published a pamphlet ridiculing Francis and had the nerve to hand him a copy while Francis was leading a religious event at his cathedral. The bishop read it and did nothing about it. Later, instead of penalizing the priest, as his friends suggested, he treated him kindly and even granted him favors.

If we think of ourselves as a nothing, as a servant of all those we meet (as did St. Francis of Assisi and St. Thérèse of Lisieux), we will embrace the hurts and humiliations

---

[17] Johannes Jorgensen, *St. Catherine of Siena*, trans. Ingeborg Lund (New York: Longmans, Green, 1942), 48. "I am who am" is the name God gave when Moses asked God his name (see Exod. 3:14).

we endure as splinters of the cross we must bear for Christ. These are sacrifices that we can joyfully accept as offerings to save souls, including our own.

This is not the same as being a doormat. A doormat is someone who has no self-esteem and thus allows the whole world to take advantage of him in every situation. A Christian is one whose self-esteem comes from sacrificing his life for Christ and his people, one who is moving in a planned direction to become a new creation in Christ. The doormat puts up with all kinds of injustices because he thinks he has no choice. A Christian endures injustices patiently because it's a spiritual work of mercy and he chooses to be an image of the One who endured the greatest injustice ever borne: death on a Cross for a world of sinners.

St. John wrote, "Who is it that overcomes the world but he who believes that Jesus is the Son of God?" (1 John 5:5). Clearly there is a sense in which we have *not* overcome the world. The world is a mess.

In another sense, however, we *have* overcome the world if we are so focused on Christ that *the world can't get to us any longer*. When Peter kept his eyes on Christ, he could walk on water, but when he began to listen to the "winds of the world," he sank (see Matt. 14:28–30). If we are truly living for Christ and we have become a new creation in his image, the world cannot get to us; it cannot ruin our peace. We shouldn't get upset while listening to the news. It's not that we don't notice the evil being done in the world, or to us in particular, or that we don't care about it. It's that we realize that in the large scheme of things, in light of the Kingdom, what is happening around us is not so important. We keep our eyes fixed on our eternal destination, where there will be no evil. I often say to those who lament the terrible state of world affairs, "Just remember, God is still in charge." And He is!

We don't disengage ourselves from the world. Not at all. We are concerned about making the world a better place and are active in doing so as Christians, but if the world — or *our* world — is not as we would like it to be, we shouldn't get angry. We should work at making it better but not lose our peace over it. Francis de Sales wrote, "If the whole universe should be convulsed, we ought not to be troubled, for the whole world is worth less than peace of soul."[18]

[18] Very Rev. George Porter, S.J., ed., *The Heart of St. Francis de Sales: Thirty-One Considerations upon the Interior Virtues of This Great Saint* (New York: Catholic Publication Society, n.d.), 7, http://www.oblates.org/dss/heart_of_desales/heart_of_desales.pdf.

Overcoming Sinful Anger

Overcoming Pride

Anger (the sin) and unforgiveness are related to pride. In essence, it is saying, "How dare you make me feel bad!" or "How dare life give me this trouble!" Pride is considered the root or beginning of all sin. I often encourage people with an anger problem to pray daily for humility. It works. This prayer, adapted from the famous prayer of Cardinal Merry del Val is what I give them:

O Jesus, meek and humble of heart,
*   make my heart like unto thine.*
From the desire to be esteemed, deliver me.
From the desire to be honored, deliver me.
From the desire to be praised, deliver me.

Teach me to accept humiliation,
*   contempt, rebukes,*
being slandered, being ignored,
being insulted, being wronged,
and being belittled.

Jesus, grant me the grace
that others be admired more than I;
that others be praised and I unnoticed;
that others be preferred to me in everything;
that others be holier than I,

provided I become as holy as I should;
that I might imitate the patience
and obedience of Your mother, Mary. Amen.

St. Augustine wrote, "If you ask me what is the most essential element in the teaching and morality of Jesus Christ, I would answer you: the first is humility, the second is humility, and the third is humility."[19] Shortly before St. Francis de Sales died, as he was leaving the Visitation sisters, the Mother Superior (St. Jane Frances de Chantal) asked him for one last piece of wisdom. He wrote three times on a piece of paper, "Humility."[20] St. Vincent de Paul wrote, "You must ask God to give you power to fight against the sin of pride, which is your greatest enemy — the root of all that is evil, and the failure of all that is good. For God resists the proud."

Humility is consistently praised in Sacred Scripture, and pride disdained:

He who is greatest among you shall be your servant; whoever exalts himself will be humbled, and

[19] Letter 118, 22.

[20] Michael de la Bedoyere, *SaintMaker: The Remarkable Life of Francis de Sales, Shepherd of Kings and Commoners, Sinners and Saints* (Manchester, NH: Sophia Institute Press, 1998), 333.

whoever humbles himself will be exalted. (Matt. 23:11–12)

He has scattered the proud in the imagination of their hearts, he has put down the mighty from their thrones, and exalted those of low degree. (Luke 1:51–52)

Humility is praised about 25 times in Scripture; the humble are praised about 48 times. Pride is held in contempt 103 times in Scripture; the proud are disdained about 68 times. If there was ever a foundational virtue to strive for, it is humility.

What can you do beyond praying for humility to arrive at this virtue? I recommend reading the lives of the saints, especially St. Francis of Assisi. He founded the Order of Friars Minor (now known as the Franciscans), with the intention of having the members seek the last and lowest places in all things, so as to follow the example of Jesus, who came not to be served but to serve.

Another saint to read about is John Vianney. When he received by accident a petition circulated by some of his jealous fellow priests accusing him of "sensationalism, ignorance, and [showy] poverty," he signed it and sent it on to the diocese. At one point he said, "I thought a time would come when people would run me out of Ars with sticks, when the bishop would suspend me, and I should end my days in prison. I see, however, that I am not worthy of such a grace."

The lives of the saints are full of such stories about humility. We should have a steady diet of reading them.

Spiritual Works of Mercy

Earlier I mentioned one of the Spiritual Works of Mercy: to endure injustices patiently. That is a key element in living a spiritual life that many Christians forget. Sure, we try to get justice, but anyone who has lived a while in this world knows that you can't always get it. Sometimes we just have to live with an injustice, and if we bear it patiently, we gain a great deal of grace.

A cousin of this spiritual work of mercy is to forgive all injuries. If we can make habits of this and of bearing injustices patiently, we will be well on our way to real holiness.

The most basic way to know that we have forgiven others is to pray for them, for their good and especially for their salvation. St. Elizabeth of Hungary once prayed to God to give great graces to those who had injured her the most. After this prayer Jesus said to her, "My dear daughter, never in your life did you make a prayer more pleasing to me than the one you have just said for your enemies; on account of this prayer I forgive not only all your sins but even all temporal punishments due to them." Let us follow the example of St. Elizabeth!

5

Heal Painful Memories

Sometimes people get stuck when they try to get over their anger or to forgive. They can't seem to erase the terrible memory. A key way to deal with this is called healing of memories. Dennis and Matthew Linn have studied the whole process of healing memories, and they suggest that there are five stages in healing a memory, similar to the five stages of facing death outlined by Elisabeth Kübler-Ross:

1. Denial: The person refuses to admit he was hurt.

2. Anger: The person blames others for hurting him.

3. Bargaining: The person puts conditions on his willingness to forgive. In other words, he decides what it would take for him to forgive. Although these conditions are usually unlikely to be met,

the offended person at least allows that forgiveness might be possible.

4. Depression: The person is down on himself for allowing this hurt to paralyze him.

5. Acceptance: The person seeks to grow from this hurt.[21]

The authors propose four emotions to be worked through to become healed: anxiety, fear, anger, and guilt. They describe the case of a woman named Margaret who was deeply hurt by being refused reentry into India, where she had been teaching as a missionary for several years.[22]

She identified her first stage, that of denial, in her dismissing the feeling that she would not be asked to return to India after coming to the United States on a vacation. She chose not to face that possibility with her superior.[23]

Her anger stemmed from the fact that her superiors had blamed their refusal to bring her back to India on the fear that she might catch malaria. Her health was excellent,

---

[21] Dennis and Matthew Linn, *Healing Life's Hurts* (Mahwah, NJ: Paulist Press, 1978), 11.

[22] Ibid., 9.

[23] Ibid., 12, 13.

and she had just passed her checkup with flying colors. It was a false excuse.[24]

Next came bargaining, and the conditions she set for herself for forgiving the offending parties. She would forgive them only if they reversed their decision, realized the harm they had caused, and became committed never to do such a thing again. They did none of these, however, and they continued to harm others in the same way.[25]

When she moved on to depression, to acknowledging her own failure in all of this, she realized it was not the offense that had caused her misery. It was her overreaction that had brought her down. Was her value tied only to this fulfilling mission in India or in her being a child of God, deeply loved by him? And now that she was a mission director, she was beginning to act just like her former boss, happy to refuse volunteers on flimsy pretexts.[26]

When she arrived at stage 5, acceptance, she began to see the benefits she had gleaned from being turned away from the missionary work she loved. She saw how this experience had moved her to a closer relationship with God and with other people. She realized that her value

[24] Ibid., 13
[25] Ibid.
[26] Ibid.

stemmed not from her work or from the opinions of others, but from her Father in heaven.[27]

She sought out a priest and went to confession. She confessed simply, "I'm sorry for being away so long, heavenly Father." She experienced a deep peace and became quite sensitive to others who were dealing with similar hurts. She warmly comforted a woman who had also been denied readmittance to India for the same mission. In fact, this was the same woman who had denied her reentry before![28]

At the peak of her misery she had contracted cancer. After being bedridden for two years with the disease, and then after healing her memories, she was able to take a full-time job counseling cancer patients—this, despite the opinion of six cancer doctors that she should have died several years before.[29]

Two things helped Margaret to heal her memories: telling her story to friends, particularly to one who had told her, "You're angry"; and telling her story to Jesus. Having heard those words from her friend, she acknowledged her anger and spoke of it to Christ. She expressed to him her

[27] Linns, *Healing Life's Hurts*, 14.
[28] Ibid.
[29] Ibid.

unwillingness to forgive her antagonist but then began to work through the other stages to final acceptance. It was suggested that had she simply said, "I forgive her" without engaging her deep anger, she might have remained at the denial stage and never achieved healing.[30]

Margaret moved slowly through the five stages, because her friends and Jesus didn't rush her. She was able to take time to move from stage to stage, and thus her healing was deep. The authors of this study, however, caution against insisting that each stage be formally experienced. It is possible to skip certain stages, according to the workings of the Holy Spirit.[31]

Anxiety, Fear, Anger, and Guilt

Margaret had gone through many sleepless nights, anxious over her situation. This anxiety was an indicator that she was "emotionally overloaded." She passed through her stage of denial to come to realize the source of her anxiety. What had made her anxious was the fact that she had to get a new job, find new friends, and pursue a whole new way of life.[32]

[30] Ibid. 15, 16.
[31] Ibid., 17, 18.
[32] Ibid., 24.

Her anxiety began to subside when she spoke with Jesus and her friends about her fear, anger, and guilt over her situation. Her main fear was that she was going nowhere; her existence was without direction. Once she identified what she was afraid of, she was ready to deal with her anger and guilt.[33]

Her anger was aimed at the boss who out of envy prevented her from returning to this job she loved in India. Her guilt stemmed from failing to act on her premonition that her missionary job might be terminated and for placing too much importance on her India activities. Life is much more than a good job.[34]

As she passed through her fear, anger, and guilt, she got to the bargaining stage. There she lowered her terms for forgiving her offending supervisor. She forgave the woman, despite the fact that she had not backpedaled at all regarding Margaret. Margaret reached the acceptance stage by seeing the good that could flow from her rejection. She realized that her importance comes from God, not from persons or from a job. And she could use her own experience to become more sensitive to others, and even to her own petty treatment of missionary volunteers. By

[33] Linns, *Healing Life's Hurts*, 24, 25.
[34] Ibid., 25.

apologizing to those volunteers, she even developed many new friends.[35]

The authors explain how the story of the disciples on the road to Emmaus provides a pattern for healing. The disciples went through anxiety, anger, fear, and guilt, and then they experienced the unconditional love and kindness of Jesus. Once he had explained the Scriptures about himself, they felt forgiven and they appreciated all they had been through. They returned to Jerusalem with their hearts healed.[36]

One final story of the many given by the Linn brothers involved a physical healing through the healing of memories of a woman called Agnes. The vision in her right eye had been growing worse for fourteen years. Her left eye was beginning to fail as well. She attended a workshop for healing of memories, where the participants prayed over her. She needed to heal the memory of her father, who had cut off all communication with her forty-five years before, when she had entered a nursing career. She tried not to think of this memory since she saw it as the root of her sad life without her father's love.[37]

[35] Ibid., 25.
[36] Ibid., 28, 29.
[37] Ibid., 30.

Overcoming Sinful Anger

On day 1, Agnes expressed to God her anger at her father's abandoning her. But she also expressed her own guilt at not having contacted her father. On day 2, she brought herself back forty-five years to the onset of the wound her father had caused and imagined God the Father embracing her in unconditional fatherly love. She felt her sadness fade as the Father continued to hold her. Then the Father held her hand and asked her to give that same loving forgiveness to her father, deceased fifteen years already at that point.[38]

On day 3, she tried to deepen her love for her father, and she tried to see what blessings she might have received from her difficult life without him. She took comfort in the way her separation had moved her to pursue a strong relationship with God through prayer and to serve patients in their loneliness for thirty-eight years.[39]

As her memory began to be healed, so did her eye! It improved gradually each day, and by the end of the workshop, she was able to read to the other participants the passage in Mark 8:22–26 about the blind man who regained his sight gradually when Jesus laid hands on him.[40]

[38] Linns, *Healing Life's Hurts*, 31.
[39] Ibid.
[40] Ibid.

Heal Painful Memories

Agnes later wrote to Fr. Linn to express her gratitude. She was very happy to have received her eyesight back, but she added, "Oh, the deep healing of memories I have had with my father is beyond any blessing I have ever experienced or expect to experience."[41]

You can use these same steps to heal your own painful memories.

1. Consider whether you are in denial that you were hurt. If you are, admit this denial so that you may move to the second step.

2. Get deeply in touch with the feeling resulting from the hurt.

3. Decide on what terms you might forgive the offender. This bargaining, of course, is not terribly virtuous, but its value is that you concede that you might indeed forgive. It is an intermediate step, which is better than the initial position of completely refusing to forgive.

4. Redirect your anger at yourself for allowing this wound to hold you back from living a productive, anger-free life.

[41] Ibid., 31, 32.

5. Acknowledge the hurt as an opportunity for growth, and identify how it has helped you develop virtue. Name the benefits you reaped from the event, especially the ability to be more sensitive to others who have been hurt.

By following these steps you will truly be able to forgive those who have hurt you, and you will find some peace about the past. In doing so, you will likely feel anxiety because this hurt has repercussions and will or could cause trouble in your life. You might go through a period of fear that you may be unable to forge ahead in your life. You might fear that this hurt will paralyze you and keep you from getting beyond this and living a productive life (especially if the hurt involved a major disappointment). You must acknowledge your anger at the person who hurt you. To deny your anger while feeling it deeply within would only delay the healing.

A necessary emotion in the process of healing is guilt over the fact that you let this bother you so much. This is not the unhealthy guilt that you hang on to long after your reform, a guilt that stems from pride. This is the healthy guilt that leads to a change in behavior, analogous to that needed for a good confession. This guilt inspires you to proceed in healing your memories and accepting that the event can be used to help you grow and become a better person.

6

Calm Marital Anger

Having worked with a good number of married couples, I have discovered that anger is a strong force for dividing husband and wife. Each spouse needs to know how to keep calm and to help the other keep calm as well.

Calming an Angry Wife

Now, when a husband has an angry wife, what can he do? One thing he shouldn't do is lose his own cool. If she expresses childlike anger, he can smile back at her, but he should be sure to tell her, "I'm sorry I made you angry. Will you forgive me?" as the man in the earlier example did. Simple enough.

If she expresses explosive anger, he should listen carefully until she is finished. Then, once he knows why she is angry, he can offer to discuss the matter. He could say, "Tell me what I did wrong, and I will try to improve."

That's often a winner. When a woman is upset, angry or not, she often wants to talk about it. He needs to listen.

One husband told me that he often could not talk about whatever the source of contention was because he was not exactly clear on why his wife was angry. I suggested he make a firm date with his wife, perhaps the next day at 5:30 p.m., to discuss the whole matter in detail. Never leave it hanging.

Calming an Angry Husband

St. Monica had a husband with a wild temper. When he got angry, she would say nothing. She would go about her business saying very little and wait until he had calmed down to speak to him. She had plenty to complain about too, since her husband was a womanizer, as were most of the husbands in Tagaste (Northern Africa) at the time. Many of her friends suffered bruises from their husbands, but Monica didn't, because she knew when to be quiet and when to speak. Best of all, she was able to facilitate the conversion of her pagan husband and his difficult mother.

Was she a doormat? No way. She knew what was important to her — her relationship with God — and she was not going to allow anything to interfere with that, even her exasperating husband.

Calm Marital Anger

It seems that silence or speaking very little—not defending oneself and not losing one's temper—is the best way to calm an angry husband. It is hard to have a rational conversation with a man who is in a rage. "Let every man be quick to hear, slow to speak, slow to anger, for the anger of man does not work the righteousness of God" (James 1:19–20). This is not the silent treatment. It is waiting out the storm, not punishing.

Once a husband gets a lot of his anger out, his wife might say, "As I read you, you're upset because of [whatever it is], right?"

And then she can try to have a rational discussion. She can ask him if he would be willing to tell her more and tell him that she really wants to understand. And, if he tells her more, she can offer him some help in the matter. *It's all about putting aside her anger at the way he's behaving and getting to the sore point and healing it.*

St. Paul of the Cross wrote, "When you feel the assaults of passion and anger, then is the time to be silent, as Jesus was silent in the midst of His ignominies and sufferings." Maintaining silence when one is angry is a good idea for both husbands and wives, but especially for wives.

7

Turn Your Anger at God to Praise

Many people get angry at God when things go wrong in their lives. "God, how could you let this happen? I thought you were supposed to be so good!" Does God let bad things happen in our lives? Yes, in a sense, he does. It's what we might call his permissive, or reluctant, will. He does not want terrible things to happen to us, but his agenda is not of this world. Everything that he permits to happen is for some greater good, some eternal good. If the only thing that mattered was for things to turn out well in this life, we might have a case against God when tragedies occur. But, *it is the eternal good that matters, and that's virtually impossible for us to figure out.*

A perfect example of that is the suffering and death of Jesus. It was a tragedy in terms of this world for Jesus, the only son of Mary and the teacher and leader of eleven good men and the Church that followed, to die on a cross.

Yet the eternal good from that event was beyond every conceivable worldly good.

Suffering is always related to some sin in the world. My suffering is not necessarily the result of my sin, but of some sin, as Pope St. John Paul II taught: "At the basis of human suffering, there is a complex involvement with sin."[42] Jesus' suffering was redemptive. Ours can be as well if we embrace it as the cross Christ promised his followers.

Jesus himself expressed frustration during his Crucifixion. He cried out the words that begin Psalm 22, thereby taking upon himself every frustration of life ever endured by us on earth:

> My God, my God, why hast thou forsaken me?
>   Why art thou so far from helping me, from the
>   words of my groaning?
> O my God, I cry by day, but thou dost not answer;
>   and by night, but find no rest.
>
> Yet thou art holy,
>   enthroned on the praises of Israel.
> In thee our fathers trusted;
>   they trusted, and thou didst deliver them.

---

[42] Pope John Paul ll, *Salvifici Doloris* (The Christian Meaning of Suffering), February 11, 1984, no. 15.

Turn Your Anger at God to Praise

> *To thee they cried, and were saved;*
> *in thee they trusted, and were not disappointed.*

> *But I am a worm, and no man;*
> *scorned by men, and despised by the people.* (1–6)

But, that psalm ends with a note of hope:

> *I will tell of thy name to my brethren;*
> *in the midst of the congregation I will praise thee:*
> *You who fear the LORD, praise him!*
> *all you sons of Jacob, glorify him,*
> *and stand in awe of him, all you sons of Israel!*
> *For he has not despised or abhorred*
> *the affliction of the afflicted;*
> *and he has not hid his face from him,*
> *but has heard, when he cried to him.* (22–24)

There is a similar dynamic in Psalm 13:

> *How long, O LORD? Wilt thou forget me for ever?*
> *How long wilt thou hide thy face from me?*
> *How long must I bear pain in my soul,*
> *and have sorrow in my heart all the day?*
> *How long shall my enemy be exalted over me?*

> *Consider and answer me, O LORD my God;*
> *lighten my eyes, lest I sleep the sleep of death;*

> lest my enemy say, "I have prevailed over him";
>   lest my foes rejoice because I am shaken.
>
> But I have trusted in thy steadfast love;
>   my heart shall rejoice in thy salvation.
> I will sing to the LORD,
>   because he has dealt bountifully with me. (1–6)

In fact, each time the psalmist complains to God, he ends by praising him (see also Ps. 35:17–18 and 42:9–11). That is a good thing to do!

So, although there is some biblical evidence that it is permissible to be frustrated with God, if not angry, the bottom line is the only reasonable conclusion: God is not to blame! God is good and worthy of our praise. How ungrateful we are to have so many gifts in life (count them sometime!) and, when we lose one gift, to get angry at God.

Thanking God

If we spent time each day thanking God, we would hardly be able to get angry at him. Instead we tend to take for granted the gifts we have. For these, we should thank God unceasingly. I composed the following prayer to remind myself and others of the many gifts we have received from God:

Turn Your Anger at God to Praise

Prayer of Thanks

Heavenly Father, I thank you for my very existence, which you gave me out of the abundance of your love and which you sustain at every moment. I thank you for my health, which I so often take for granted, for my parents and family, which I also take for granted. I thank you for my intellect, by which you gave me the power to think, and for my will, by which you gave me the power to love. Thank you for my body, and the food and drink by which you sustain it, and the shelter by which you protect it. Thank you for my soul and for your word and sacraments, by which you nourish it.

My every talent comes from you, my every possession, my every moment of time, for which I will be eternally grateful. Thank you for Blessed Mary, who intercedes for me always. And thank you most of all for Jesus, who has given us new life, new hope, new love by his death and Resurrection, and for the Church, which brings him to me each day.

What an awesome, generous, loving God you are!

You ask me to honor and worship you at least weekly and to pray to you without ceasing. It is my joy to do so in thanksgiving for all you have given me. Amen.[43]

If our youth would say that prayer daily, they might never ask the question, "Why do I have to go to Mass every Sunday?" or "Why should I pray?" If we would pray that prayer daily, we might never become angry at God.

God's Will

Also, when people pray hard for something and don't get it, they sometimes get angry at God. It seems we think we can manipulate God with our prayers, and if we pray hard, we think he *must* provide whatever we ask for. God answers *every* prayer, but sometimes the answer is no. And, if it *is* no, we're better off—if we love God. That's why Jesus wants us to say, "Thy will be done" in the Our Father. That is the sure way to happiness—the will of God. This belief is an essential part of our Christian faith.

Some go through a short-lived frustration with God. The Scriptures seem to allow for that. But the person who stays angry at God betrays a lack of knowledge of God. If we have an intimate relationship with him, there is no way

[43] This prayer is available at the Catholic Faith Alive! website, http://www.cfalive.com/online-store/miscellaneous/.

we can become angry at him, because we have a deeply intuitive knowledge of his goodness and his personal concern for our happiness.

Praising God

An excellent way to avoid getting angry at God is to praise him for everything. Methodist minister Merlin Carothers happened upon this way to deal with irritating events in his life. He began to praise God for all that happened to him, good or bad. This was based on Romans 8:28: "We know that in everything God works for good with those who love him, who are called according to his purpose." So, he reasoned, if we love God, no matter what happens, good will come of it.[44]

He praised God when he had a car problem and was sent to a repair shop known for overcharging people. He went there and had to make an appointment to come the next day for his car to be looked at. He kept praising

[44] Carothers wrote about all this in his "praise books," especially his first book, *Prison to Praise* (Escondido, California: Merlin R. Carothers, 1970; eighteen million copies in print!), in which he describes the many miracles that occurred for those who trusted enough to praise God always.

God through it all. As he started his car and began to leave, the mechanic told him to shut it off so he could try something under the hood. After he had fiddled with it for a few minutes, he told Carothers to try starting it again. The problem was fixed. He asked the mechanic how much he owed him, and the mechanic replied, "Not a thing, sir."

He got a soldier and his wife (Carothers was a military chaplain) to praise God even though the wife was suicidal over her husband's being sent to Vietnam. She had been adopted and was estranged from her family. She couldn't bear the idea of being alone, without her husband. Within a few days after they (reluctantly) praised God for their situation, the wife met a soldier out of the blue whose mother turned out to be her own mother. All of a sudden she had a mother and a brother. Meanwhile, her husband was able to have his orders changed, and stay in the United States. She now had a family *and* a husband at home. Praise God!

To praise God for even the apparently bad things that happen is to trust him, and God loves trust. He told St. Maria Faustina (the Divine Mercy saint), "The graces of my mercy are drawn by means of one vessel only, and that is trust. The more a soul trusts, the more it will receive. Souls that trust boundlessly are a great comfort to me, because I pour all the treasures of my grace into them."[45] He also told her, "Sins of distrust wound me most painfully."[46]

There's more to praising God for trials experienced. It's found in Colossians: "Now I rejoice in my sufferings for your sake, and in my flesh I complete what is lacking in Christ's afflictions for the sake of his body, that is, the church" (1:24). In a sense, of course, there is nothing lacking in Christ's sufferings for the Church. For the infinite dimension of sin, the offense against God, Christ had to pay the whole debt, since we could never make a dent in that. But for the finite dimension, the harm done to ourselves and the world, we are to make up for at least part of it ourselves. That is what St. Paul was speaking of.

And that is what St. John of the Cross was saying when he asked God to allow him to suffer something each day for Him. It is what Teresa of Ávila had in mind when she wrote, "Let me suffer or let me die." It is what St. Thérèse was thinking of when she suffered her final illness and said, "I would not want to suffer less," because it was her

---

[45] St. Maria Faustina, *Divine Mercy in My Soul, The Diary of the Servant of God, Sister M. Faustina Kowalska* (Stockbridge, MA: Marian Press, 1987), no. 1578.
[46] Ibid., no. 1076.

"desire to save souls." And it is part of the message of Mary to the children of Fátima when she asked, "Do you want to offer yourselves to God, to endure all the suffering he may send you, as an act of reparation for the sins by which He is offended, and to ask for the conversion of sinners?" (They said yes, by the way.)

What is the message of saints such as Padre Pio who have the stigmata, the wounds of Christ in their hands and feet? Is that a privilege? Of course it is! So the message is that sharing in the redemptive suffering of Christ is an honor. If we embrace our crosses rather than cursing them, we do share in Christ's work of redemption.

It is difficult to lose your temper when you are praising God for the good that will come of whatever tragedy you are faced with and for the chance to share in the redemptive mission of Christ. St. James wrote, "Count it all joy, my brethren, when you meet various trials, for you know that the testing of your faith produces steadfastness" (James 1:2–3).

8

Learn to Overcome
Your Habit of Anger

Is reform possible? Absolutely. And it's even likely that the committed Christian can overcome his anger. Several saints did it.

St. Francis de Sales had quite a temper when he was young. When older, as bishop of Geneva, he was known for his mildness and patience. Even though he was very busy, no one ever felt rushed in his presence. When St. Jane Frances de Chantal encouraged him to be a bit angrier over the opposition they were facing in starting their religious order, he replied, "Would you have me lose in a quarter hour what has taken me twenty years' hard work to acquire?"[47]

[47] Rhonda Chervin, *Taming the Lion Within* (Oldsmar, FL: Simon Peter Press, 2003), 37.

Overcoming Sinful Anger

St. Thérèse of Lisieux had a terrible temper as a child. In her mother's words: "[Thérèse] flings herself into the most dreadful rages when things don't go as she wants them. She rolls on the ground as if she's given up hope of anything ever being right again. Sometimes she's so overcome that she chokes." Later Thérèse learned to control her temper and use this energy to love God and her neighbors in the convent, a few of whom were anything but lovable.[48]

St. Vincent de Paul was another reformed grump. He said that "without the grace of God he would have been 'hard, repulsive, rough and cross.' "[49]

St. Jerome is said to have had an irascible personality. He made so many enemies in Rome by his nasty criticisms that his enemies tried to bring him down. He had to flee Rome to get away from their treachery and eventually ended up in Bethlehem, where he began to live a life of penance. Even there, however, he got into heated exchanges of ideas with his (former) friend Rufinus and with the Pelagians.

[48] St. Thérèse of Lisieux, *The Story of a Soul: The Autobiography of St. Thérèse of Lisieux*, trans. John Beevers (Garden City, NY: Image Books, 1957), 13.
[49] Joseph Esper, *Saintly Solutions to Life's Common Problems* (Manchester, NH: Sophia Institute Press, 2001), 4.

Learn to Overcome Your Habit of Anger

Although he often alienated people by his harsh wit, Jerome was known for being always ready to seek pardon for his temper. Pope Sixtus V once remarked, regarding a picture of Jerome beating his breast with a stone, "You do well to carry that stone, for without it the Church would never have canonized you."

Blessed John Columbini had a terrible temper. This fourteenth-century merchant was also known for his greed. One evening he became furious because his meal was not ready when he arrived home. His wife handed him a book on the saints, which he promptly flung to the floor. Having done so, he was ashamed of his childish behavior, so he picked up the book and began to read it. He was so fascinated by what he read that he forgot about his dinner. This was the beginning of his conversion. He gave away much of his fortune, made a hospital out of his home, and began to take care of a leper himself. And, of course, he conquered his temper.[50] Reading about the saints can be a great antidote to unrestrained anger.

How to Change with God's Grace

The first step toward change for the Christian is to seek God's grace. The most fundamental way to seek grace is

---

[50] Ibid., 4–5.

prayer. Meditation on the life of Christ, by way of the Rosary or just meditating on Sacred Scripture is an excellent way to draw closer to Christ and to imitate in some ways the life he led. In fact, the Lord told St. Maria Faustina, "There is more merit to one hour of meditation on My sorrowful Passion than there is to a whole year of bloody scourging." What patience the Lord showed in his Passion!

Certainly the sacrament of Reconciliation is an important element to overcome sins, especially sins of anger. This is true not only for the grace we receive from this sacrament, but also the frequent calling to mind of our sins. Biweekly confession could be an important practice to overcome deep-seated sins.

Participating in the Holy Mass, perhaps daily, is the greatest source of grace we have, and receiving the Lord in the Eucharist whenever we attend Mass can be a powerful antidote for anger.

Holy Communion separates us from sin. The body of Christ we receive in Holy Communion is "given up for us," and the blood we drink is "shed for the many for the forgiveness of sins." For this reason the Eucharist cannot unite us to Christ without at the same time cleansing us from past sins and preserving us from future sins.... As bodily nourishment restores lost strength, so the Eucharist strengthens our charity, which tends to be weakened in daily life; and this living charity *wipes away venial sins*. By giving himself to us Christ revives our love and enables us to break our disordered attachments to creatures and root ourselves in him. (CCC, nos. 1393, 1394)

To be sure, not only do we need to seek God's help in curbing our angry behavior, but if we would draw close to him, we must bring graciousness and kindness into the depths of our being. St. Francis de Sales wrote:

When there is nothing to stir your wrath, lay up a store of meekness and kindliness, speaking and acting in things great and small as gently as possible. Remember that the Bride of the Canticles is described as not merely dropping honey, and milk also, from her lips, but as having it "under her tongue" [Song of Sol. 4:11]; that is to say, in her heart. So we must not only speak gently to our neighbor, but we must be filled, heart and soul, with gentleness; and we must not merely seek the sweetness of aromatic honey in courtesy and suavity with strangers, but also the sweetness of milk among those of our own household and our neighbors; a sweetness terribly lacking to some who are as angels in public and devils at home!"[51]

We might assume that most people who are struggling with their anger are not thinking of how they can be "filled heart and soul with gentleness," but that should be our goal. Mildness, as a fruit of the Holy Spirit, should go deep if we want to become the people Jesus wants us to be. It won't be easy to show mildness to others if our hearts are churning with harshness. To remove a diseased tree, we must take it out by the roots.

Other Methods to Help You Change

Happily, as a supplement to the key ingredient of grace, some experts have developed effective methods to overcome anger (and many other bad behaviors as well). In their book *Change Anything*, authors Kerry Patterson, Joseph Grenny, David Maxfield, Ron MacMillan, and Al Switzler claim that most people don't overcome their bad habits because they rely solely on willpower. They must utilize a good number of other tools to overcome their

---

[51] St. Francis de Sales, *Introduction to The Devout Life*, pt. 3, ch. 8, http://www.catholictreasury.info/books/devout_life/dev52.php.

propensity to overeat, or to overspend, or for our purposes, to explode in anger.[52] They spell out a series of steps to bring about desired change.[53]

Prepare for the Battle

The first step is to identify times when you are liable to get angry. Is it when you arrive home after work, or when your son refuses to obey you, or when your wife undermines your authority? Whatever the situations are, you must identify them so you can be ready to contain your ire when these situations come up.

Then, you must map out how you are going to respond to these situations in the future. For example, if you usually get angry when you get home from work, you should plan on the way home just how you are going to react to whatever you have faced before that incited your anger. If it is your disobedient son who stirs you up, you must figure a better way to handle that. Perhaps you will promise a

---

[52] The authors do not deal specifically with the problem of uncontrolled anger, but their ideas can easily be used to deal with this problem.

[53] From Kerry Patterson, Joseph Grenny, David Maxfield, Ron MacMillan, and Al Switzler, *Change Anything: The New Science of Personal Success* (New York: Business Plus, 2011), 31–43.

punishment if he doesn't comply, and you will deliver that message calmly but strongly.

It may be that you are angry at home because something unpleasant occurred at work or while you were driving home. It is important to recognize such past behaviors and tell yourself how unjust that is. It is surprising to hear how many people act angry at home for something that happened at work.

Next, see how you can apply various sources of self-influence to the problem of your anger (these will be discussed below). Finally, any time you fail to accomplish your goal of staying calm for that day, review what happened and use that information to determine how not to fail in the future. In other words, feed this information into step 1 (when you identify times you are liable to get angry) as a piece of data you need to plan for, in case the same situation arises again.

Ways to Influence Your Behavior

There are many ways to self-influence your behavior to make it easier to change. It often just won't do just to say to yourself, "I *will* to change, and so I'll do it." For most people that isn't enough.

• Consider your future. One key way to change your behavior is to work out in your mind just what your life will be like if you don't change your angry behavior. Suppose you blow up two or three times a week. What might your life be like twenty or thirty years from now if you don't change? There's a good chance you'll be divorced, your children will dislike—if not hate—you, and they will probably grow up with an anger problem to share with their family.

Imagine you are living alone in an apartment (child support and perhaps alimony as well can be expensive). Imagine that your loving relationship with your spouse has turned into bitterness or at least apathy. Imagine your life on Thanksgiving and on Christmas. You might like to spend these days with your children, but they won't want a raging bull with them on a holiday. And, of course, imagine your children having a miserable marriage because of their anger. In other words, consider in detail what your "default future" might be if you don't change.[54]

Meditating and reflecting on what will be the long-term results of continuing your anger is a bit like cognitive therapy. In that process, you constantly remind yourself of the benefits to be gained, and the harm to be avoided, by changing your behavior. You straighten out your thinking so as to correct your inclination to do evil. Working

[54] Ibid., 55–56.

with those trying to overcome unchastity, I have had them make a list of the benefits of chastity and read it several times a day. This is based on the teaching of Aristotle, St. Thomas Aquinas, and Pope St. John Paul II. In many cases it has worked well, producing ongoing chastity in those struggling with this virtue.[55]

If you struggle with an anger problem, write on an index card all the negatives of continuing your anger, and read that list several times a day. It might look something like this:

Reasons to Overcome Anger

1. If I don't change I will harm my marriage and perhaps end up divorced.

2. If I can't calm my anger, my children may grow up to fear and hate me.

3. If they see me angry often, my children may develop the same anger problem in their marriages.

4. With continued anger and unforgiveness, I will increase my chances of heart disease and cancer [as we saw earlier].

[55] See my book *Achieving Chastity in a Pornographic World* (New Hope, KY: New Hope Publications, 2007).

5. Anger could harm my ability to keep a job.

6. Anger hurts my relationship with God.

On the back of the card you might add this little quote from St. Catherine of Siena:

It is because anger and impatience are the very pith and sap of pride that they please the devil so much. Impatience [a close cousin of anger] loses the fruit of its labor, deprives the soul of God; it begins by knowing a foretaste of hell, and later it brings men to eternal damnation: for in hell the evil perverted will burns with anger, hate and impatience.... There is no sin or wrong that gives a man such a foretaste of hell in this life as anger and impatience.[56]

Read the card several times a day until you are totally convinced that your anger will never make you happy. It might take a few months or even longer. But, once your heart and head are going in the same direction, you should be able to conquer your angry behavior without a struggle when provoked.

[56] Vida D. Scudder, ed., *Saint Catherine of Siena as Seen in Her Letters* (London: J. M. Dent and Company, 1905), 37.

• Self-control is a good thing to have when pursuing a more peaceful way of coping with unpleasant events. But self-control is not a full virtue, since, as Aristotle said, with a true virtue, you do the good joyfully, easily, and promptly. In a sense, you retrain your appetite to avoid going after sinful activity.

• *Consider the person of peace you could become.* We are encouraged to use "value words." Your curbing your anger is not making you less of a person or harming your ability to control others, but it is turning you into a true gentleman or a true lady, helping you become a person of peace, and, of course, helping you to be a witness for the peace of Christ.[57]

Know Your Abilities

This source of influence involves taking an inventory of your skills in regard to your problem. Do you know how to control yourself, or do you give in to every emotion that comes along? Do you know how to be calm when things in life heat up? Do you know how to get your children to obey by offering them incentives? Do you know how to compensate for your bad moods?

[57] Patterson et al., *Change Anything*, 56–58.

Learn to Overcome Your Habit of Anger

Identify the skills you need and then practice them with a friend, who will be your "coach." For example, have your coach play the role of your daughter when you want her to do something. What sort of incentive could you come up with to inspire her to obey, an incentive short of blowing your stack? What is it that she likes that you might threaten to take away? Perhaps her computer game or her phone. What would she value as a positive incentive, something you could give her if she completes the task you're asking of her? Perhaps a special movie night or a trip to the ice cream shop.

Suppose your coach helps you practice by playing the role of your wife and undermining your authority. What would you say to her? Would you go crazy, or would you say, "We had better talk about this later"? You may have to make a firm date for that talk, but that beats losing your cool.

Beware of Enabling Friends

Enablers in this context are those who help you to do what you are trying not to do. The accomplices of an angry person might be his family. Perhaps his father or mother or his whole family have had problems with explosive anger and still do. Well, if he wants to overcome his own anger, he should not spend too much time in that atmosphere. He is just asking for trouble if he mixes it up with them often.

On the flip side, it can help to have a friend who is peaceful to calm you down. St. John Bosco was used to settling things with his fists and his strength when he was young. Then he met a new student by the name of Luigi Comollo. When one student threatened to hit him if he didn't join in their boisterous game, Luigi politely declined. When the boy did hit him, Luigi said, "Are you satisfied? Now go in peace. I have already forgiven you."

Bosco immediately made friends with Luigi, seeing in him the example of gentleness John wanted. When some time later the boys started picking on Luigi, John picked up one of the boys and swung him around, sending four boys to the floor and the rest running for cover.

Luigi later counseled John, "I am amazed at your strength. But God didn't give you strength to wipe out your friends. His will is that we should love one another, forgive one another, and return good for evil."[58] John knew he was right, and he was delighted to have the influence of such a friend.

[58] St. John Bosco, *Memoirs of the Oratory of St. Francis de Sales from 1815 to 1855*, trans. Daniel Lyons, S.D.B. (New Rochelle, NY: Don Bosco Publications, 1989), 79.

Learn to Overcome Your Habit of Anger

Sometimes you can turn acquaintances into helpers by simply discussing with them what you are striving for. Tell them what kind of support you would like in order to accomplish your goals.[59]

Provide Incentives for Yourself

Imagine this: if every time you behaved a certain way — in our case, got unreasonably angry — you lost $1,000, you might be much more motivated to change. (In fact, divorce reduces a person's net worth by 77 percent.[60])

It seems that short-term incentives work better than long-term ones. One young man had a number of long-term incentives provided by his boss for taking special classes to improve his computer skills, but he needed more. So he provided himself smaller incentives for each week he attended class and did the homework: he would take his girlfriend out to one of his favorite restaurants. That's what pushed him to complete the classes and excel in his job.[61]

But it seems that we are more motivated by the risk of losing something than we are by the prospect of gaining

---

[59] Patterson et al., *Change Anything*, 94–95.

[60] J.L. Zagorsky, "Marriage and Divorce's Impact on Wealth," *Journal of Sociology* 41, no. 4 (2005): 406–424, as found in Patterson et al., *Change Anything*, 102.

[61] Patterson et al., *Change Anything*, 103–104.

something. One man who needed more motivation to go regularly to the gym hired a fitness coach to work with him. Missing a day at the gym would not have bothered him much, but wasting the money he was paying for the fitness coach would have bothered him a good deal, and that kept him going to the gym.[62]

In trying to change, we should use smaller, short-term incentives rather than larger, long-term ones. Some years back, a famous actress was given a large monetary incentive for each pound she lost. She lost the weight, but once she reached her goal, what happened? She put the pounds back on. A large incentive can become the main reason for change but once it is gone, so is the good behavior. So short-term incentives are better than long-term ones.[63]

I tried this myself recently. I wanted to get rid of a bad habit, so I put ten one-dollar bills into a coffee mug. Each day I avoided the bad habit, I took a dollar out. Each time I failed, I put two dollars in. If the amount in the mug increased to twenty dollars, I would give ten to the poor. Within four days, my habit was almost completely wiped out! So what's a dollar to me or to you? Not very much. Nonetheless, knowing the money was there and knowing

[62] Patterson et al., *Change Anything*, 106.
[63] Ibid., 107–108.

the consequences of my behavior gave me sufficient motivation to overcome a habit I had not been able to beat. My interest in winning the "game" helped keep me aware of the goal.

Fresh from that success, I tried it on the task of cleaning my room for ten minutes a day. This time the penalty for failing would be three dollars. I had not been able to make that a habit for thirty years. I missed only *once* in the first five weeks. It worked, big time!

So, if your problem is anger, you might try the same sort of thing. Perhaps put twenty dollars into a cup, take out one dollar on each day you don't lose your cool, and put in five each time you get angry. If the total goes to thirty or forty, give all but twenty to the poor. The psychological benefit of this little trick is amazing.

Provide Reminders

It often helps to place little reminders in strategic places. Perhaps you can post small signs saying "kindness" or "patience" or "peace" around your home to remind you to work on these virtues. If you want to be cryptic simply place small cards with the letter *K* or *P* in strategic places.

Or you could do as one woman did: place a list of things to do differently on the dashboard of your car, and read through it before entering your house. It could include a reminder to take some deep breaths and think of one reason you are grateful for your spouse or for the child who makes you angry.

Some business leaders had a history of becoming angry when dealing with problems that arose in meetings. The company installed mirrors on their office doors. When the leaders had to confront a problem, they stopped at the mirror to see if they looked angry. If so, they did some deep breathing and carried out some anger management techniques.[64]

Good preparation, self-awareness, short-term incentives, and reminders are effective tools in changing habits. Give them a try, and you might soon find yourself finally overcoming your anger.

[64] Patterson et al., *Change Anything*, 123, 134.

9

Help Your Children
Overcome Their Anger

What do you do with a child who is often out-of-control angry? The first thing to remember is to stay calm and don't get into the shouting. Always respect your child; never insult him or call him names.[65]

If you assign a punishment right away, make sure it is a just one, not too severe. Therapists recommend you walk away for a time before assigning a punishment, unless you are needed to separate fighting siblings. If you have already given a warning with a punishment attached, of course, you need not delay the ruling. If you

[65] Material from this paragraph and the subsequent two are from Tim Murphy and Lorainn Hoff Oberlin, *The Angry Child* (New York: Three Rivers Press, 2001), 35, 36, 40.

do delay, you need to come back shortly and address the problem.

It is important to punish your child if appropriate, but at the same time you must keep loving him. One of our youth-group members ran up a $2,000 bill on her cell phone one month, and her father was livid. She told me, "I can pay the $2,000 in time, but I wish he wouldn't stop talking to me for two weeks." You may take away privileges as punishment, but don't make yourself unavailable.

You must remind your children that it may be "okay to be angry, but it is never okay to be mean."[66] Lyman Abbott put it similarly: "Do not teach your children never to be angry; teach them how to be angry." And, Aristotle wrote, "Anybody can become angry—that is easy—but to be angry with the right person and to the right degree and at the right time and for the right purpose, and in the right way—that is not . . . easy."

You as a parent should apologize if you did something wrong in a conflict and be always ready to forgive your child. If you made mistakes in the conflict, figure out how not to make them again the next time an explosion occurs. Experts recommend calling a family meeting to discuss the

[66] Murphy and Oberlin, *The Angry Child*, 40.

issue. That can give children a feeling of ownership for their family and their behavior.[67]

What are some things parents can do to help their child rein in his anger? The first thing is to offer encouragement. Words such as "I know you can overcome this behavior, and I'm willing to help you" can have a powerful effect on a child.[68] I once told a seventh grader with poor performance in school, "I know you're not stupid. In fact, you're smart. Once you learn how to study, you'll do well." He got 100 on his next test, and I announced it to the whole class. He went on to do well in eighth grade and got into a good high school. A bit of encouragement for a youth can go a long way.

Work at developing ways to get your child to talk about things. Perhaps take him out to breakfast some Saturday and talk about a lot of things before talking about the anger. In other words, build a friendship before bringing up the topic of anger.[69] And when you do talk about things, discuss some better ways for him to deal with the situation. Help him to identify his feelings and how to express them constructively. Point out the harm done by his behavior,

[67] Ibid., 41.
[68] Ibid., 47.
[69] Ibid., 49.

and encourage him to think about how his behavior affects other people.[70]

Some children use anger to dominate their parents. And sometimes parents allow this by not disciplining their children for fear of that anger. Parents must learn how to discipline their children while maintaining their own dignity and respect for their child.[71] I have encouraged some parents to say, "I hate to have to punish you for this, but I would be a bad parent if I didn't."

Identifying the Source of Children's Anger

Author Douglas Riley proposes several issues that cause children to explode in anger. The most common issue, according to him, is the "road map meltdown." This means that a child is anticipating a certain sequence of events to occur in the near future, and all of a sudden the sequence changes. He thought his mom was taking him to Walmart, and she decides she needs to stop at the drugstore first. He can't deal with the change, so he explodes in anger.[72]

---

[70] Murphy and Oberlin, *The Angry Child*, 64, 65.

[71] Ibid., 65–67.

[72] Douglas A. Riley, *What Your Explosive Child Is Trying to Tell You* (New York: Houghton Mifflin, 2008), 5, 6.

Another issue behind children's blowups is defiance. Defiant or oppositional children are more focused on power. They want to show that no one can make them do what they don't want to do. They want to wield as much power as their parents. This category is quite different from the "road map meltdown" child and calls for a different approach for reform, which I'll discuss shortly.[73]

Allergies and sensitivities to foods can also be important factors behind childhood anger. Many of the children referred to Dr. Riley for anger problems have dark circles under their eyes, "ruddy ears or cheeks, a chronic runny nose, a history of ear infections, or a history of bouncing off the walls after consuming certain foods or food additives."[74]

A friend of mine had suddenly become quite irritable with her roommate and others. It took her several weeks to discover that she was allergic to her laundry detergent! Once she changed that, her irritability vanished. Likewise, I suffered incessant colds at one point, until discovering that I was allergic to the detergent used for my sheets.

My allergist once told me that the number-one symptom for allergies was an inability to sleep at night. It made perfect sense, given what I was going through. If a child

[73] Ibid., 6, 7.
[74] Ibid., 7.

is tired all the time, he will have difficulty coping with difficult situations, and angry blowups may follow. Lack of sleep, with or without allergies, can be a trigger for anger in children.

Anxiety and depression are two other possible factors that underlie explosive behavior in children, according to Riley, as can attention deficit hyperactivity disorder (ADHD) and bipolar disorder. Immaturity, lack of communication skills, and learning disabilities can be a source of frustration for children, and thus a trigger for anger.[75]

Overbooked families create stress that can lead to anger in their children. If children are going in every different direction for soccer practice, basketball practice, music lessons, and chess club, they will be overstressed, and so will their parents. And stress often leads to anger. Psychologist Tim Murphy observed that one family was happy to come for counseling because he insisted that all cell phones and pagers be turned off. This was the only time the families experienced peace in their lives. If a family wants less anger, they must schedule more family time and fewer outside activities and distractions.[76]

[75] Riley, *What Your Explosive Child Is Trying to Tell You*, 8, 9.

[76] Murphy and Oberlin, *The Angry Child*, 89.

Help Your Children Overcome Their Anger

An angry family is one in which the parents set the awful example of being angry much of the time. They teach by their example that anger brings power. It should go without saying that parents should work on their own behavior before they can expect their children to change.[77]

An indulgent family is one in which one or both parents want peace at any price. That is invariably too expensive. Parents must learn that they are responsible for teaching their children that anger doesn't pay. They do this by punishing bad behavior and rewarding good. Sometimes this is a whole lot of work, but it has to be done. If not, problems get worse and worse. If parents bite the bullet and discipline their children, they will save a good deal of time and effort in the future.

How to Help

For children with road map meltdowns, Dr. Riley recommends using the "big kid" approach. When a child behaves well, he is a big kid. Rewards are "big kid treats": big kid ice cream cones, big kid brownies, and so forth.[78]

---

[77] Ibid., 90–94.
[78] Riley, *What Your Explosive Child Is Trying to Tell You*, 24, 25, 27–29.

Riley also suggests a variation on this: the "big kid brain" and the "little kid brain." He tells children they have two brains, and each is trying to be the "boss brain." Then he plays a game with them. He plays the role of the little brain, and the child plays the role of the big brain.[79] He begins by saying something like, "Mom wants us to stop watching TV and come for dinner. No way. Let's blast her!" The child may respond (as Mr. Big Brain), "No, let's not. We'll be punished." Little Brain (Riley) responds, "Who cares! Let's cause a stink." The child answers, "No, we're going to act big," and so forth. Riley uses a lively, silly voice and makes it great fun. He lets the child, the big brain, win in the end and gives him a high five. The children love it.[80] Riley says this works well for three- to six-year-olds, but older children may balk at it. If this method fails, he proposes praising the children whenever they behave well. He also promises children rewards—really good rewards—if they make an effort to do better.[81]

Another technique Riley suggests to overcome road map meltdowns is "exposure therapy." This involves slowly

[79] Riley, *What Your Explosive Child Is Trying to Tell You*, 28, 29.
[80] Ibid., 29, 30.
[81] Ibid., 32, 33.

exposing the child to road map changes so as to desensitize him. He begins with a simulation, role playing with the big brain and the little brain when a change of plans occurs. Then the parent explains that she is going to do a real situation in which she changes the plan in the middle and promises the child a reward if he can get through it well. That is the basic method. Riley has some caveats to fine-tune this, but that is the gist of his approach. He provides examples of how this approach has been most effective with some children.[82]

For defiant children Dr. Riley suggests another approach entirely. Defiant children are trying to win the authority battle with adults and have no desire to change, as do the road map meltdown kids. He emphasizes that parents should remain totally calm and cool and avoid getting drawn into children's arguing snare. Here he relies heavily on punishment and rewards, with the emphasis on rewards. He encourages few warnings about punishments, and taking away only enough privileges to get the child's attention, no more.[83]

Riley told one wildly defiant nine-year-old girl that there was good news and bad news. She asked for the

[82] Ibid., 39–47.
[83] Ibid., 85–88.

bad first, so he obliged. He told her about losing TV, cell phone, and iPod privileges, favorite clothes, snacks, and so on. He said he didn't like the punishment route for bad behavior but greatly preferred the reward route for good behavior.[84] Then he launched into the rewards. He said he realized that changing behavior was hard work and thus should be rewarded very well. Not just well, but very well. He described some of the possible rewards as a trip with her friends to the amusement park; a night at the movies with her friends, popcorn and all; shopping and an amazing lunch at the mall. She was hooked. She said she was definitely interested in option 2![85]

Riley's approach seems very wise, very positive: small punishments, large rewards.

Some parents are not so sure about all these rewards. They want their children to behave well because it's the right thing to do. However, the reward and punishment approach just anticipates how the world will treat them, and how it is in life generally. You do evil, you lose out. You do good, you receive rewards. It's that way at work, with friends, with spouses, with everyone. In time, kids

---

[84] Riley, *What Your Explosive Child Is Trying to Tell You,* 89, 90.

[85] Ibid., 90, 91.

come to realize that life is better if they behave well, and they see the intrinsic value of doing so, but many kids, probably most kids, begin with rewards and punishments.

Another point that Riley makes is to help children be aware of the effect of their behavior on others, especially parents. A parent will ask, "How are you making me feel now by your behavior?" When the child says, "I don't know," as many will, the parent says something like, "Well, if you didn't have access to your Xbox for a while, perhaps you could come up with an answer to that."[86]

When it comes to allergies, Dr. Riley encourages parents to bring their children for testing if necessary. Some allergists doubt that allergies could be the cause of children's explosions. Riley suggests that parents avoid such allergists — or, I would say, those who just talk about allergies, not behavior.[87] In any case, allergies can be very stressful for people of all ages. Some of the more common allergens are milk products (my allergist told me that 80 percent of those who suffer from allergies are allergic to milk products), wheat, peanuts, pollen, mold, dust, and of course, detergents (many brands now offer a "free and clear" version without any scents or other allergens). I

[86] Ibid., 94, 95.
[87] Ibid., 56, 57.

always seal off the mattress and box spring on my bed since in the past I suffered terribly from an allergy to dust mites.

My allergist urged me to give up refined sugar, and refined flour products. When I did, I felt so much better that I never went back. Riley proposes a food elimination diet to check for food allergies. To do this, you eliminate a suspected food, such as milk products, for four days. Then you reintroduce the food and observe the results. If there are no bad symptoms, assume that that food is not the culprit.[88]

Riley proposes treatment for the other possible underlying problems in angry children mentioned earlier. He covers ADHD, anxiety disorders, obsessive compulsive disorder (OCD), bipolar disorder, depression, learning disabilities, sensory processing disorder (SPD—difficulty processing sensory data), and sleep disorders. All of these can be at the root of childhood anger. If your child might have any of these—or any of the above-mentioned problems—I recommend Dr. Riley's book, *What Your Explosive Child Is Trying to Tell You*. This is the most practical book I have found on childhood anger.

---

[88] Riley, *What Your Explosive Child Is Trying to Tell You*, 69–71.

Help Your Children Overcome Their Anger

Angry children can make us so irritated that we may become irrationally angry ourselves. So it is important that we help them find their way to overcome their anger and find peace.

10

Summary

In summary, the most toxic anger generally comes in three forms: passive-aggressive, blowups, or perpetual. In passive-aggressive anger, the person doesn't lose his temper; he just gets even by subverting the efforts of the person who made him angry.

The person who blows up does so most often for one of three reasons: power and control; refusing to take responsibility, or habit. In the first, the person tries to control others by getting angry when they don't conform to his wishes. In the second, the person pretends he has no choice but to lose his cool when others cross him. (Wrong.) In the third, the person has grown up with anger and is so used to it that he can't conceive of a life without anger. Of course, all three are not acceptable behavior for a Christian.

The third type of anger, perpetual anger, is found in the person who cannot find a way to cope with a disappointment and so is furious much of the time. This person needs to come to the realization that he is ruining his life by failing to process the disappointment and must find a way to get beyond it. The healing of memories can be most useful in doing this.

To process anger rationally, we must first determine if what we are angry about is significant. If it isn't, we need to drop it. If it is, we need to decide whether speaking to the person who made us angry will do any good. If we think it will, we should speak diplomatically to that person and request better behavior. If it won't do any good, we need to give it to God as a sacrifice for sin. And, we may need to do this repeatedly.

There are three actions a Christian can take to overcome sinful anger. First, he must forgive. This is not an option for the true Christian—he must forgive in order to be forgiven, in order to be saved. Second, he can see whatever has made him angry as his cross, something he can bear, to make reparation for sins and to save sinners. Third, he can trust that "in everything God works for good with those who love him" (Rom. 8:28). As such, he can learn to praise God for all things, good or bad, confident that some good will come of them.

If we have an angry child, it's important to work to help him get beyond that anger. There are known practical methods to aid in this task. In particular, offering incentives—good and bad—can be most effective.

And children are not too young to realize the value of accepting, even embracing their cross. The mother of St. Paul of the Cross used to hold up a crucifix and ask Paul if he could suffer this for Christ as Christ had suffered for us. It was not just a way of dismissing his sorrow and getting him to quiet down. It was something she believed and by which she lived.

My own mother did something similar. She taught me about the cross and the need to accept and bear crosses as a sacrifice to God. When I asked one day at the age of eight, "Why do I have to go to Mass on Sunday?" she answered, "It's a sacrifice." I don't know if she meant it was my sacrifice to go, or that it was the reoffering of Jesus' sacrifice on the cross. I took it as the former, and never questioned it again. (What a great mother!)

Being frustrated or angry with God may be understandable, but is futile in the end. The more we know God, the less likely we will ever be angry with him.

Anger can mean a feeling that, as something we did not will, is not sinful. Or it can mean an irrational losing of our temper, and that is sinful. If we give in to the latter, we will make those around us miserable, we will destroy relationships, and we will be more at risk for cancer and heart disease. But, worst of all, we will be doing great harm to our relationship with God.

To overcome anger we have many more tools than just willpower. There are many techniques that can help us to accomplish the changes we are trying to bring about in our lives. Overcoming anger should be a paramount change we should strive for as Christians. We should use every tool we can to help us bring about a life of peace and, as a result, a life of grace.

About the Author

Fr. Morrow has a doctorate in Sacred Theology from the Pope John Paul II Institute for Studies on Marriage and Family. He has three other books in print: *Christian Courtship in An Oversexed World*, *Be Holy*, and *Who's Who in Heaven*. His work may be found at www.cfalive.org.

Sophia Institute

Sophia Institute is a nonprofit institution that seeks to nurture the spiritual, moral, and cultural life of souls and to spread the Gospel of Christ in conformity with the authentic teachings of the Roman Catholic Church.

Sophia Institute Press fulfills this mission by offering translations, reprints, and new publications that afford readers a rich source of the enduring wisdom of mankind.

Sophia Institute also operates two popular online Catholic resources: CrisisMagazine.com and CatholicExchange.com.

Crisis Magazine provides insightful cultural analysis that arms readers with the arguments necessary for navigating the ideological and theological minefields of the day. *Catholic Exchange* provides world news from a Catholic perspective as well as daily devotionals and articles that will help you to grow in holiness and live a life consistent with the teachings of the Church.

In 2013, Sophia Institute launched Sophia Institute for Teachers to renew and rebuild Catholic culture through service to Catholic education. With the goal of nurturing the spiritual, moral, and cultural life of souls, and an abiding respect for the role and work of teachers, we strive to provide materials and programs that are at once enlightening to the mind and ennobling to the heart; faithful and complete, as well as useful and practical.

Sophia Institute gratefully recognizes the Solidarity Association for preserving and encouraging the growth of our apostolate over the course of many years. Without their generous and timely support, this book would not be in your hands.

www.SophiaInstitute.com
www.CatholicExchange.com
www.CrisisMagazine.com
www.SophiaInstituteforTeachers.org